Nursery Rhyme Crafts

Written and illustrated by Susan True

Publisher: Roberta Suid
Editor: Carol Whiteley
Design and Production: Susan True
Cover art: Corbin Hillam

ISBN 0-912107-33-2

Printed in the United States of America

9 8 7 6 5 4 3 2 1

Introduction

In *Nursery Rhyme Crafts,* you'll find easy-to-do projects that nurture imagination and self-confidence, accompanied by the nursery rhymes that inspired the projects. These simple, appealing activities will help children to practice important small-motor skills, develop sound work habits, and learn the joy of solving problems.

The easier activities come first, followed by gradually more challenging ones. All, however, are designed to promote independent work. Your role as guide will consist of reading the poems aloud (for inspiration) and modeling new techniques. Encourage experimentation and point out that there is no one "right" way to complete a task. Then, stand back unless the young craftsperson seems frustrated.

There is, of course, one more way for you to be involved. Your honest and enthusiastic reactions to finished products will play a crucial role in building motivation and skills. The more specific you are, the better. Rather than pouring out general applause—"That's wonderful!"—try focused comments: "I like the way you firmly attached the bow" or "Those three colors catch my eye." Think of the kind of feedback you like to receive and you'll know what children need.

Contents

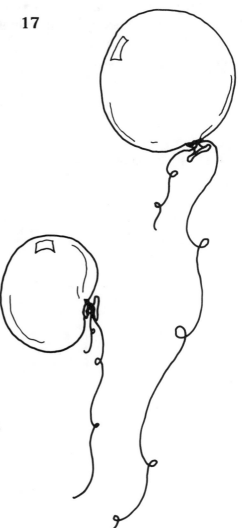

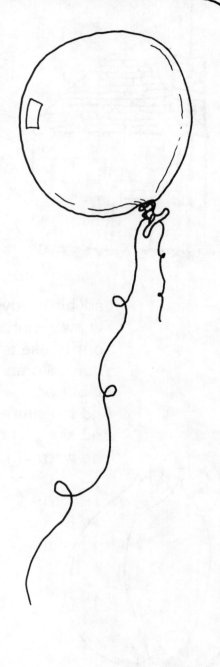

Ladybird

Ladybird, ladybird,
Fly away home,
Your house is on fire
Your children all gone;
All but one,
And her name is Ann,
And she has crept under
The warming pan.

Paperweight

Let the children decorate nice smooth rocks to resemble little ladybirds.

You Will Need:
smooth, small rocks
pieces of felt (some cut in wing shapes)
glue
non-toxic felt-tip markers
scissors

Here's What To Do:
1. Give each child one rock, several felt pieces, glue, and markers.
2. Have the children create their own ladybirds by gluing the felt wings to the rock and decorating with the markers.

The ladybirds won't be able to fly away home, but they can be taken home and used as unique paperweights!

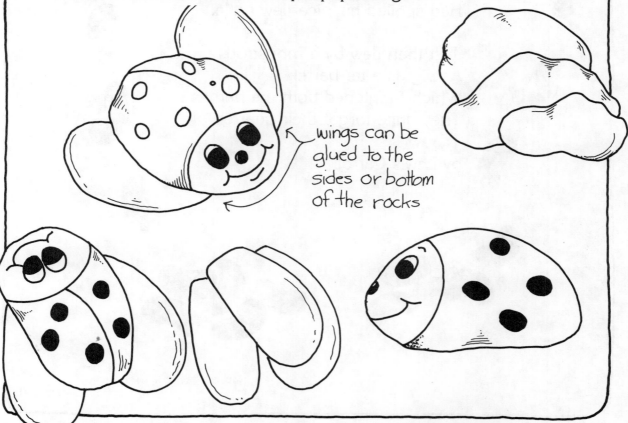

wings can be glued to the sides or bottom of the rocks

Tweedledum and Tweedledee

Tweedledum and Tweedledee
Resolved to have a battle,
For Tweedledum said Tweedledee
Had spoiled his nice new rattle.

Just then flew by a monstrous crow,
As big as a tar-barrel,
Which frightened both the heroes so,
They quite forgot their quarrel.

by Lewis Carroll

Rattle

Have the children collect plastic egg-shaped panty hose containers from their families or neighbors and let them make their own rattles.

You Will Need:
plastic egg-shaped containers
masking tape
non-toxic felt-tip markers
beans or small pebbles

Here's What To Do:
1. Give each child one plastic egg, a few beans or pebbles, and a piece of tape.
2. Ask the kids to put the beans/pebbles inside the egg, put on the top section, and secure the two halves with the masking tape (taping may require adult help).
3. Let the children decorate their eggs with the felt-tip markers.

Rattles will add fun to the next class sing-a-long.

reassemble egg after beans have been added

add tape to secure, then decorate

Humpty Dumpty

Humpty Dumpty sat on a wall,
Humpty Dumpty had a great fall;
All the King's horses and all the King's men
Couldn't put Humpty together again.

Decorated Egg

Here's a chance for the kids to design their own Humpty Dumptys.

You Will Need:
unshelled hard-boiled eggs (have a few extras in case of breakage)
non-toxic felt-tip markers
fabric scraps
small paper water cups
food coloring (optional)
scissors

Here's What To Do:
1. Cut out and discard the bottom of each paper cup.
2. Give the children time to decorate their eggs with the markers and fabric scraps; they may dip their eggs if you provide food coloring.
3. Have the children place their Humpty Dumptys in the inverted paper-cup stands.

place decorated egg in inverted cup

eggs can be decorated with scraps of felt or material

Simple Simon

Simple Simon met a pieman,
Going to the fair;
Says Simple Simon to the pieman,
Let me taste your ware.

Says the pieman to Simple Simon,
Show me first your penny;
Says Simple Simon to the pieman,
Indeed I have not any.

Simple Simon went a-fishing,
For to catch a whale;
All the water he had got
Was in his mother's pail.

Simple Simon went to look
If plums grew on a thistle;
He pricked his fingers very much,
Which made poor Simon whistle.

He went for water in a sieve
But soon it all ran through;
And now poor Simple Simon
Bids you all adieu.

Fishing Game

After the children complete this activity, they can use the paper whales they make in a fishing game.

You Will Need:
pail
sticks or dowels
assorted colors of construction paper
magnets (one or more depending on how many fishing poles
    you use)
string
paper clips
scissors

Here's What To Do:
1. Have the children cut several whales from the construction paper and attach a paper clip to each (provide a simple whale pattern if necessary).
2. Help the kids tie a piece of string to one end of their stick and attach a magnet to the other end of the string.
3. Put the whales in the pail and let your anglers start fishing (each color of construction paper can be worth a certain number of points if the children want to keep score).

attach paper clips →

attach a piece of string to the pole and a magnet to the string

Hickory, Dickory, Dock

Hickory, dickory, dock,
The mouse ran up the clock,
The clock struck one,
The mouse ran down,
Hickory, dickory, dock.

Walnut Mouse

In this activity the children make the little mouse that ran up the clock. If they like, it will follow them around the room.

You Will Need:

marbles	glue
walnut shells	non-toxic felt-tip markers
felt scraps	scissors
black yarn cut into 3″ lengths	string (optional)

Here's What To Do:

1. Give each child one marble, half a walnut shell, one piece of yarn, and some felt scraps.

2. Have the children cut ears from the felt pieces and glue them to one end of the shell. Then have them glue the yarn length to the other end of the shell for a tail.

3. Let them add eyes, nose, and mouth with the markers.

4. Finally, show the children how to put a marble under the shell and push the mouse to make it scurry. If they attach a string with a bit of glue to the shell they can pull the mouse along.

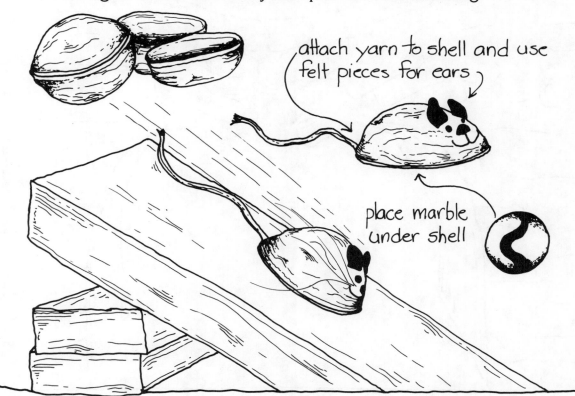

attach yarn to shell and use felt pieces for ears

place marble under shell

London Bridge

London Bridge is falling down,
  Falling down, falling down,
London Bridge is falling down,
  My fair lady.

Build it up with wood and clay,
  Wood and clay, wood and clay,
Build it up with wood and clay,
  My fair lady.

Playdough and Toothpick Bridge

The children might choose to build individual bridges or group together for a larger bridge construction.

You Will Need:
playdough
toothpicks and/or Popsicle sticks
marbles, bottle caps, small rocks, nuts, bolts, etc.

Here's What To Do:
1. Give each child some playdough and toothpicks or Popsicle sticks.
2. Encourage the children to be creative in the construction of their bridge, joining playdough and sticks as they build.
3. The kids may decorate their bridges as they like. Some might want to make cars as well, using bottle caps as wheels.

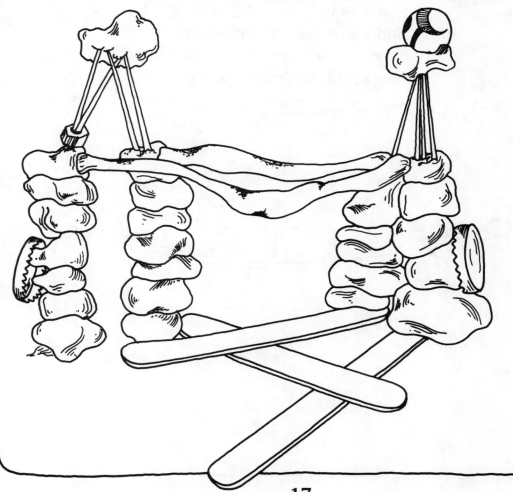

The Lion and the Unicorn

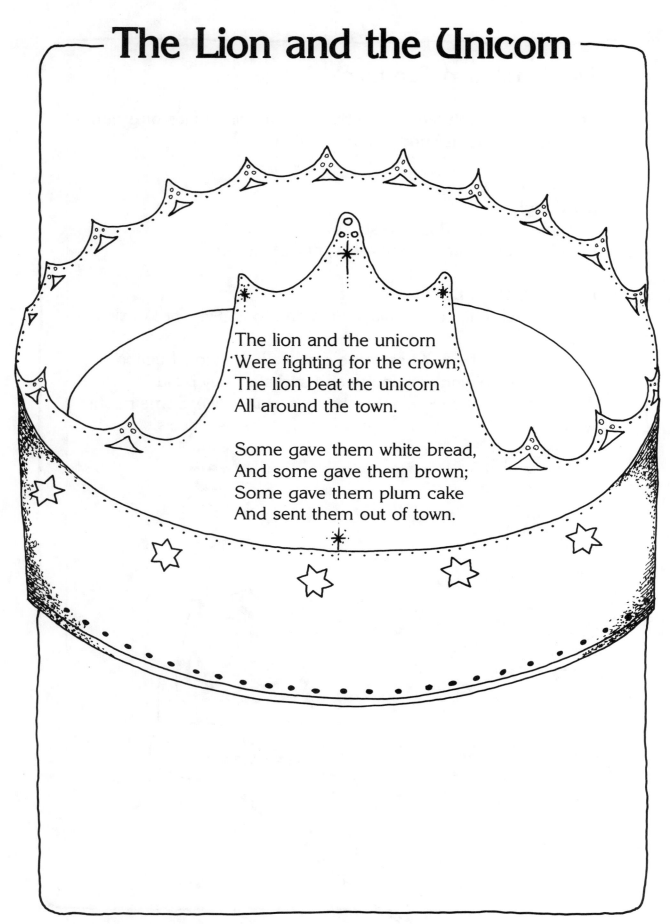

The lion and the unicorn
Were fighting for the crown;
The lion beat the unicorn
All around the town.

Some gave them white bread,
And some gave them brown;
Some gave them plum cake
And sent them out of town.

Crown Construction

Help the children make their own uniquely colored or decorated crowns.

You Will Need:
construction paper cut into 2″x26″ strips
foil cut into 4″x26″ strips
non-toxic felt-tip markers
stapler
glue
scraps of colored construction paper
narrow strips of tissue paper

Here's What To Do:
1. Give each child a strip of construction paper and a strip of foil.
2. Help the kids fit the construction paper around their heads like a headband. Have them remove the headbands, keeping the right size, and staple the overlapped ends to join.
3. Let the children wrap their headbands with foil. The crowns can then be worn as they are or decorated with additional pieces of colored construction paper, markers, or tissue paper strips attached as streamers.

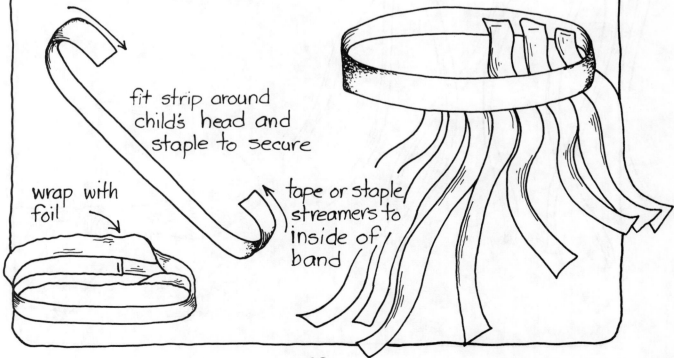

fit strip around child's head and staple to secure

wrap with foil

tape or staple streamers to inside of band

Little Miss Muffet

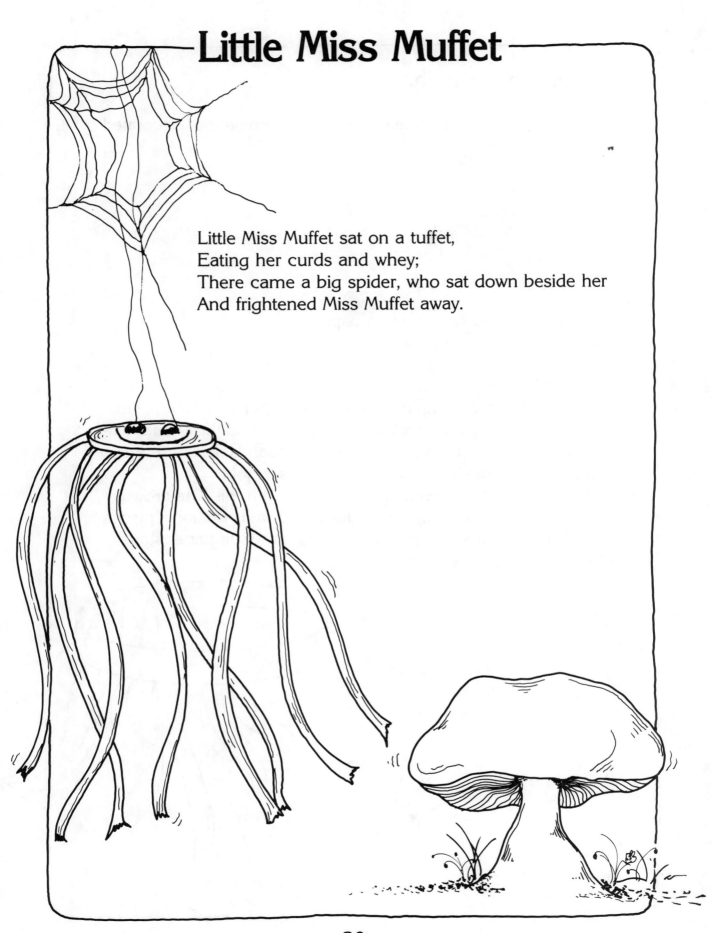

Little Miss Muffet sat on a tuffet,
Eating her curds and whey;
There came a big spider, who sat down beside her
And frightened Miss Muffet away.

Button Spider

This activity gives the children a good chance to discuss the differences between spiders and insects.

You Will Need:
black yarn cut into 4″ lengths
assorted large buttons each with 4 large thread holes
black thread

Here's What To Do:
1. Give each child one button, four lengths of yarn, and a length of thread.
2. Have the children thread two pieces of yarn through one hole and out the other so that the yarn extends equally from both holes. Have the kids repeat this step for the two remaining holes.
3. Now have the children put one end of the thread through one of the holes and knot it underneath the button. The spider is ready for dangling!

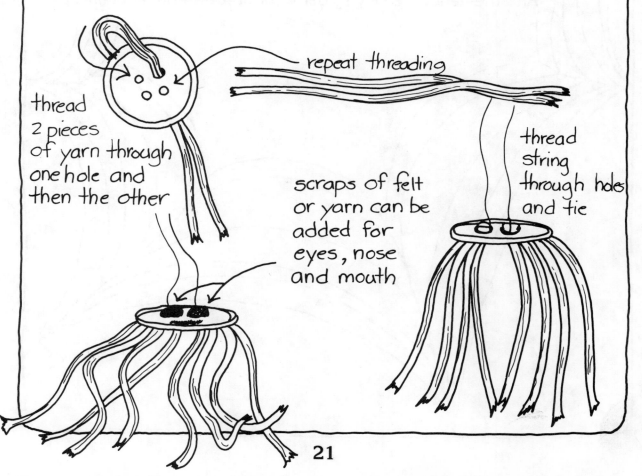

thread 2 pieces of yarn through one hole and then the other

repeat threading

thread string through holes and tie

scraps of felt or yarn can be added for eyes, nose and mouth

The Eency Weency Spider

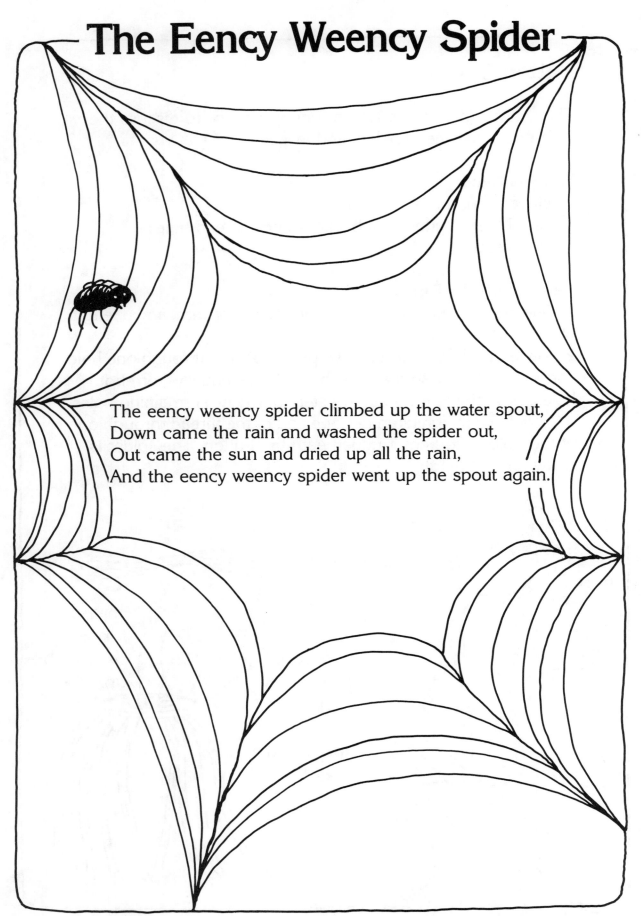

The eency weency spider climbed up the water spout,
Down came the rain and washed the spider out,
Out came the sun and dried up all the rain,
And the eency weency spider went up the spout again.

Spider Web

The spider the children made in the "Little Miss Muffet" activity can now be given a home.

You Will Need:
black yarn or heavy black string
colored construction paper
diluted glue in small containers

Here's What You Do:
1. Give each child a length of yarn, a piece of colored construction paper, and some diluted glue to share.
2. Have the children dip the yarn in the glue.
3. Let the children remove the yarn from the glue and arrange the yarn in a web pattern on the construction paper.

Once the yarn has dried, the children can dance their button spiders around on the construction paper and eventually let them rest in their new homes.

GLUE

Mistress Mary

Mary, Mary, quite contrary,
How does your garden grow?
With silver bells and cockle shells,
And pretty maids all in a row.

Paper and Foil Flowers

The children might enjoy making their own flowers to create their own bouquets.

You Will Need:
tissue paper in a variety of colors, cut into 2″ squares
foil cut into 2″ squares
green pipe cleaners

Here's What To Do:
1. Give each child at least two squares of tissue paper or foil and one pipe cleaner.
2. Have them twist each square of tissue or foil as shown.
3. The pipe cleaner stem is attached by wrapping it around the center of the two pieces of twisted tissue.

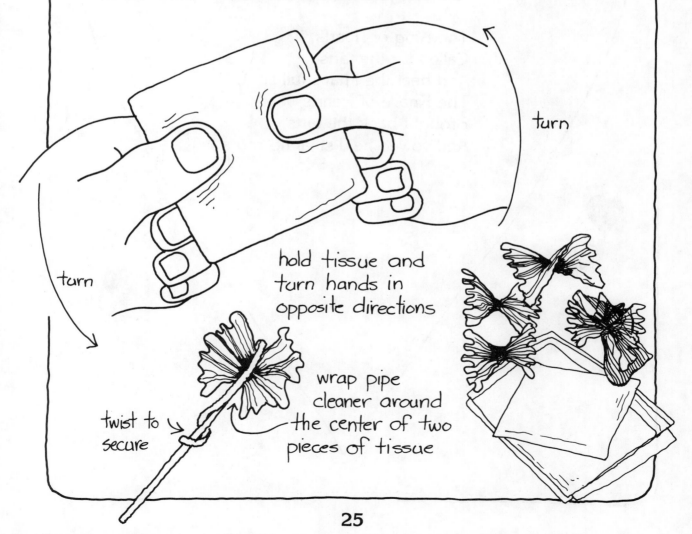

turn

turn

hold tissue and turn hands in opposite directions

twist to secure

wrap pipe cleaner around the center of two pieces of tissue

The Queen of Hearts

The Queen of Hearts
She made some tarts,
All on a summer's day;
The Knave of Hearts
He stole the tarts,
And took them clean away.

The King of Hearts
Called for the tarts,
And beat the knave full sore;
The Knave of Hearts
Brought back the tarts,
And vowed he'd steal no more.

Heart Necklace

Help the children make heart-shaped necklaces to keep for themselves or to give away as presents.

You Will Need:
baker's clay (see recipe on page 29)
paint or non-toxic felt-tip markers (optional if using colored clay)
crayon shavings (optional)
blunt nails
colorful yarn cut into 16″ pieces

Here's What To Do:
1. Give each child a small piece of clay and a length of yarn.
2. Have each child roll and shape the clay to resemble a heart (encourage the children to be creative with their clay shapes). For additional color and decoration, kids may sprinkle on crayon shavings before baking.
3. Show the children how to use a nail to make a hole in the top of their heart for the yarn to be threaded through.
4. Bake at 200 degrees for five to ten minutes. Let the hearts cool before the children string them with yarn.

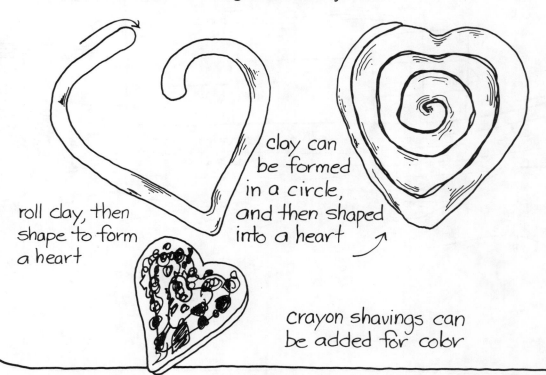

roll clay, then shape to form a heart

clay can be formed in a circle, and then shaped into a heart

crayon shavings can be added for color

The Ship's Treasure

I saw a ship a sailin',
A sailin' on the sea,
And oh, it was laden
With pretty things for thee.

There were comfits in the cabin,
And apples in the hold;
The sails were made of silk,
And the masts were made of gold.

Four and twenty sailors
That sat upon the deck,
Were four and twenty white mice
With chains about their necks.

The captain was a duck,
With a packet on his back;
And when the ship began to move,
The captain cried "Quack! quack!"

Pasta Jewelry

Talk with the children about the treasure described in the poem, mentioning the different types of jewelry the ship was laden with. Then help the kids create their own pieces of jewelry.

You Will Need:
baker's clay (see the recipe below)
food coloring (3 or 4 colors)
various shapes and sizes of pasta
oven

Here's What To Do:
1. Make up a batch of baker's clay. To make it, combine one cup flour with one cup salt and enough water to give the clay the consistency of playdough. Divide the clay and add a different food coloring to each part.
2. Give each child a few chunks of different colored clay and some pasta pieces (pasta can be colored or used as it is).
3. Encourage the children to create different pieces of jewelry by combining the clay and the pasta.
4. Bake the jewelry at 200 degrees for five to ten minutes.

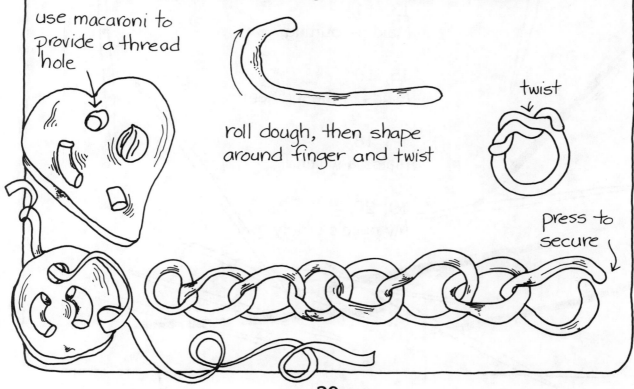

use macaroni to provide a thread hole

roll dough, then shape around finger and twist

twist

press to secure

One, Two

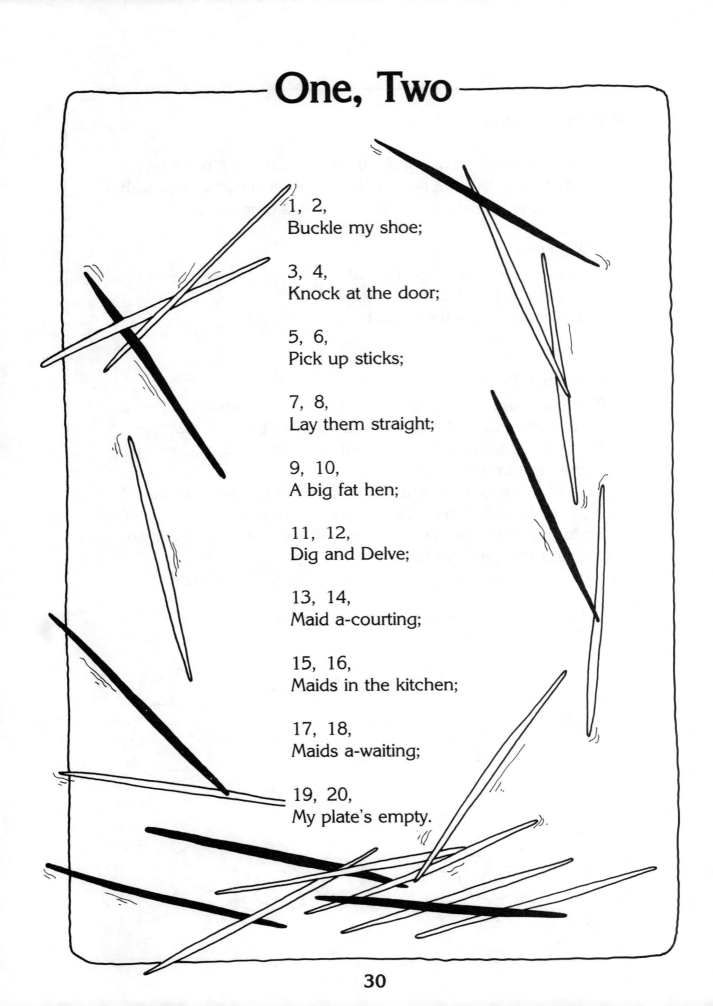

1, 2,
Buckle my shoe;

3, 4,
Knock at the door;

5, 6,
Pick up sticks;

7, 8,
Lay them straight;

9, 10,
A big fat hen;

11, 12,
Dig and Delve;

13, 14,
Maid a-courting;

15, 16,
Maids in the kitchen;

17, 18,
Maids a-waiting;

19, 20,
My plate's empty.

Pickup Sticks

This pick-up-sticks activity can be used throughout the year.

You Will Need:
toothpicks or Popsicle sticks
food coloring (3 colors)
water
jars (one for each color)

Here's What To Do:
1. Mix a few drops of each color with some water separately in each of the jars.
2. Add five toothpicks to each jar (you may do this or let the children), leaving five toothpicks natural. Remove the colored sticks and let dry.
3. Let the children play Pickup Sticks. A different number value can be assigned to each color stick or the children can take turns seeing who can pick up all the sticks without moving any others.

add toothpicks to jars

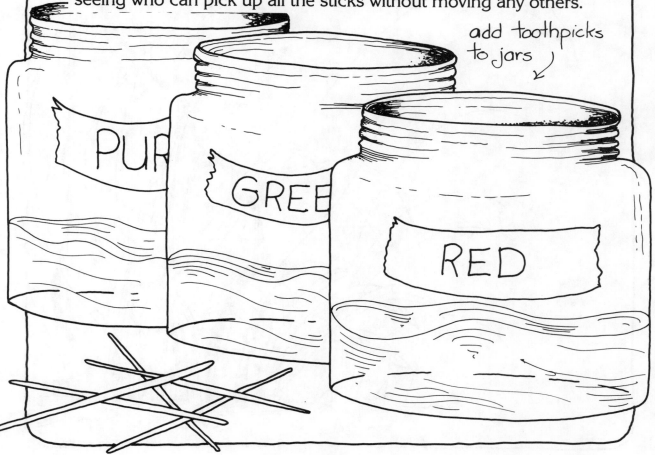

Catkin

I have a little pussy,
   And her coat is silver gray;
She lives in a great wide meadow
   And she never runs away.
She always is a pussy,
   She'll never be a cat
Because she's a pussy willow!
   Now what do you think of that!

Pussy Willow Branch

Help the children make their own pussy willows.

You Will Need:
cotton or cotton balls
glue
colored construction paper

Here's What To Do:
1. Give each child a sheet of colored construction paper on which you have drawn a tree branch. Also give each child some cotton and a small amount of glue.
2. Have the children take small pieces of cotton, about ⅛ of a cotton ball, and twist them with two hands into the approximate shape of a pussy willow catkin.
3. Let the children dip their cotton catkins in the glue and press them along the branch.

Variation: Children can use a whole cotton ball instead of pieces and decorate the ball with yarn and felt to look like a cat.

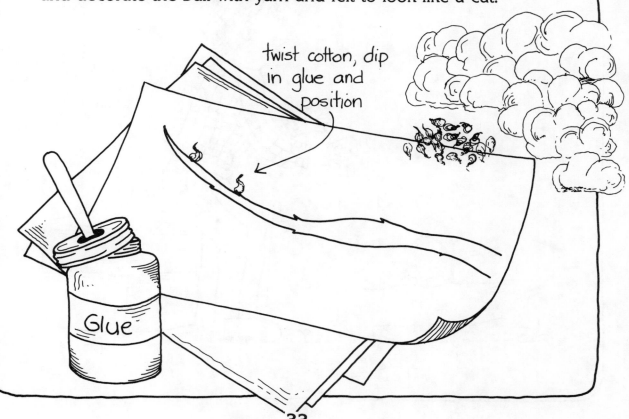

twist cotton, dip in glue and position

Glue

The Young Farmer of Leeds

There was a young farmer of Leeds.
Who swallowed six packets of seeds.
　　It soon came to pass
　　He was covered with grass
And he couldn't sit down for the weeds.

Seed and Sponge Creation

Seeds will sprout in any number of sponge creations.

You Will Need:
sponges
scissors
non-toxic felt-tip markers
seeds (alfalfa, grass, etc.)
water

Here's What To Do:
1. Cut the sponges into a variety of sizes and shapes.
2. Give each child a sponge to decorate with the markers.
3. Have the kids sprinkle seeds on the top of their sponge and add water. A circular shape, for example, could be decorated with a face and seeds sprinkled on the top to sprout into hair.

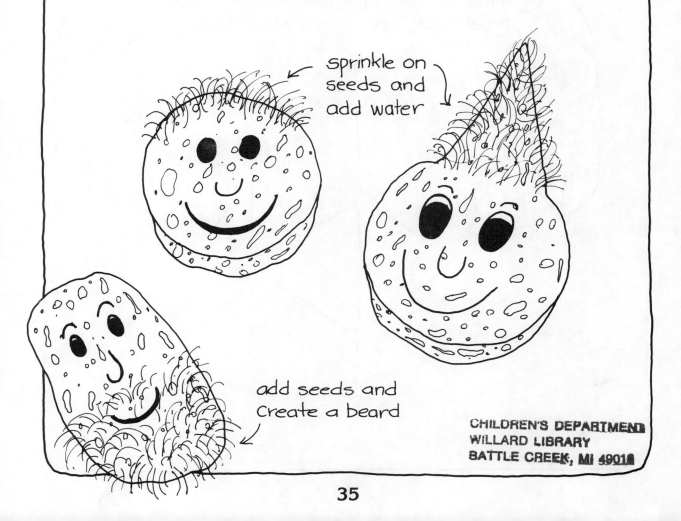

sprinkle on seeds and add water

add seeds and create a beard

Hush Little Baby

Hush, little baby, don't say a word,
Papa's going to buy you a mocking bird.

If the mocking bird won't sing,
Papa's going to buy you a diamond ring.

If the diamond ring turns to brass,
Papa's going to buy you a looking-glass.

If the looking-glass gets broke,
Papa's going to buy you a billy goat.

If that billy goat runs away,
Papa's going to buy you another today.

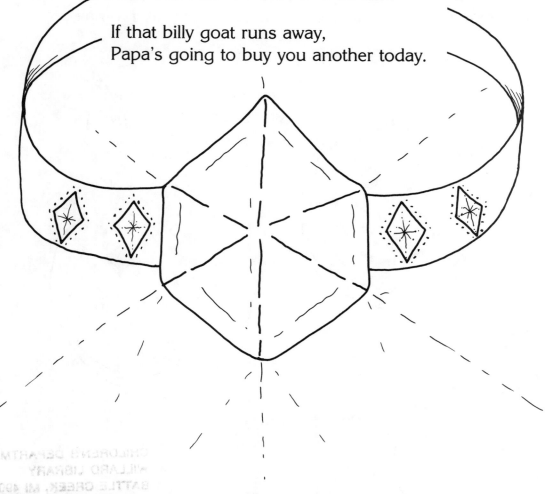

Foil Ring

A variety of decorative materials can make these rings quite attractive. Children may want to keep their rings or exchange them with each other.

You Will Need:
foil cut into 4″ squares
scissors
non-toxic felt-tip markers
sequins, glitter, or other decorative material
glue

Here's What To Do:
1. Give each child a piece of foil rolled as shown (foil can be fringed before rolling for a larger finished "stone").
2. Have the children wrap the foil around a finger and twist ends to join (the fringed piece can be "fluffed" at this point).
3. The ring can then be finished by dipping the "stone" in glue and glitter, decorating it with felt-tip markers, or twisting it and wearing as is.

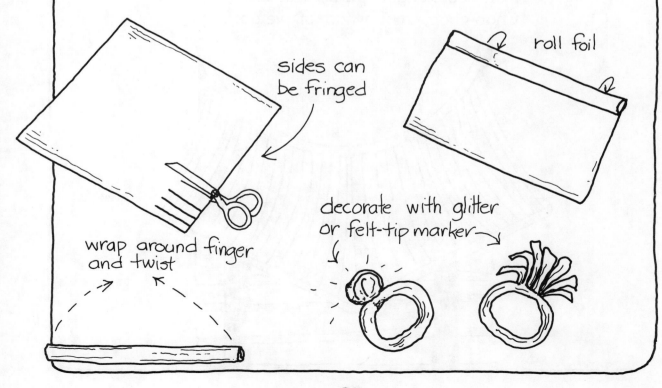

sides can be fringed

roll foil

wrap around finger and twist

decorate with glitter or felt-tip marker

The Early Morning Train

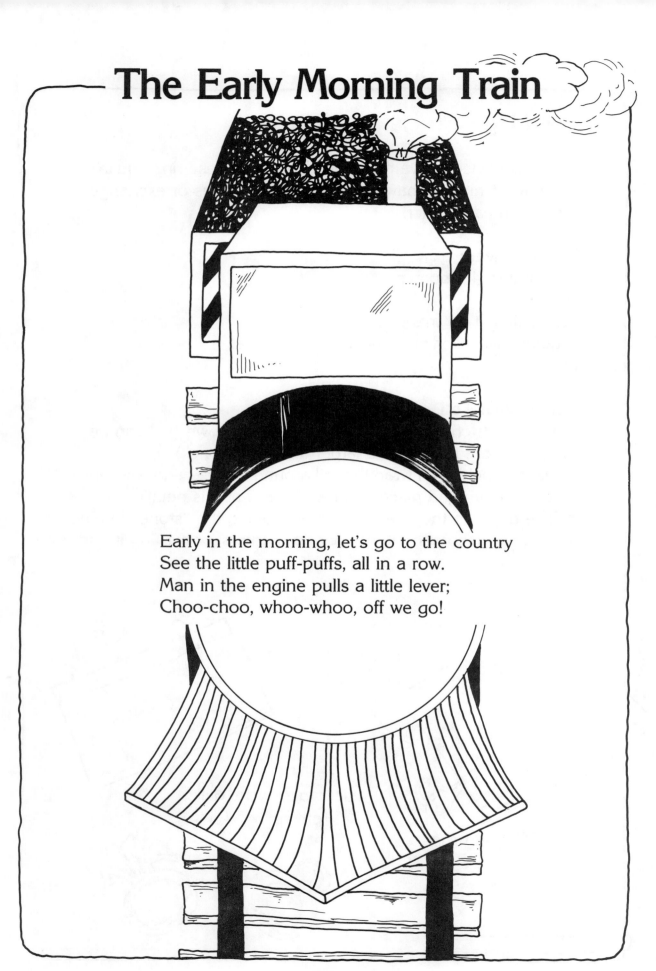

Early in the morning, let's go to the country
See the little puff-puffs, all in a row.
Man in the engine pulls a little lever;
Choo-choo, whoo-whoo, off we go!

Train Construction

After the children make a train, they can take turns being the conductor and blowing the whistle or "choo-chooing" around the room.

You Will Need:
assorted small boxes (approximately 4"x2"x2")
large thread spools (2 per train car)
unsharpened pencils
paper punch
crayons or non-toxic felt-tip markers
paper clips (optional)

Here's What To Do:
1. Give each child two pencils, two spools, and one box.
2. Help the children punch four holes in each box as shown.
3. Show the kids how to insert a pencil through the hole on one side of the box, through the spool, and out the hole on the other side of the box. Have them repeat the process for the second set of holes.
4. Let the children decorate their boxes with crayons or markers.
5. Train cars can be connected by punching holes in the front and back of each car and clipping them together as shown.

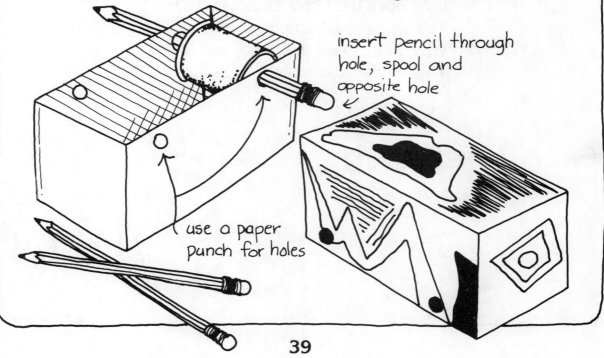

insert pencil through hole, spool and opposite hole

use a paper punch for holes

Mary Had a Little Lamb

Mary had a little lamb,
Its fleece was white as snow;
And everywhere that Mary went
The lamb was sure to go.

It followed her to school one day,
That was against the rule;
It made the children laugh and play
To see a lamb at school.

And so the teacher turned it out,
But still it lingered near,
And waited patiently about
Till Mary did appear.

Why does the lamb love Mary so?
The eager children cry;
Why, Mary loves the lamb, you know,
The teacher did reply.

Paper Puppet

The kids can carry these lamb puppets in a pocket or a purse.

You Will Need:
paper (8 ½"x11")
cotton balls
crayons
paper scraps
glue

Here's What To Do:
1. Give each child one piece of paper, several cotton balls, some crayons, paper scraps, and glue to share.
2. Ask the children to fold the paper lengthwise in thirds as shown.
3. Next, have them fold the paper in half lengthwise, then fold each end back toward the fold as shown.
4. The children can now draw faces and glue on the cotton balls and paper scraps to complete their "little lambs."

open up folded piece and bring each end to the center fold

fold in half

center

fold paper lengthwise (2 folds)

insert fingers in top section and thumb in bottom section

Here Is the Church

Here is the church, and here is the steeple;
Open the door and here are the people.
Here is the parson going upstairs,
And here he is a-saying his prayers.

Finger Puppets

The church the children create can be temporary if the kids decorate their fingers. It will be more permanent if they decorate Popsicle sticks or tongue depressors.

You Will Need:
non-toxic water-soluble markers
lots of little fingers (or Popsicle sticks or tongue depressors)

Here's What To Do:
1. Have the children draw faces on their finger tips to represent the people in the church. One finger can have a black base to represent the preacher.
2. Show the children how to intertwine their fingers to create the church and steeple, then how to reverse their hands, allowing all the "people" to show.

If Popsicle sticks or tongue depressors are used, have the kids stand in a group holding their people. The church and steeple are created when two children stand in front of the group, arms raised and hands touching.

all the
people

the
steeple

An Old Woman

There was an old woman tossed up in a basket,
Seventeen times as high as the moon;
Where she was going I couldn't but ask it,
For in her hand she carried a broom.

Old woman, old woman, old woman, said I,
Where are you going to up so high?
To brush the cobwebs off the sky!
Shall I go up with you? Aye, by-and-by.

Broom Construction

Help the children make small brooms and encourage them to repeat the rhyme as they dust around the room.

You Will Need:
tissue paper or newspaper
short sticks or dowels
tape
scissors
non-toxic felt-tip markers (optional)

Here's What To Do:
1. Have the children fringe tissue paper or newspaper as shown and then wrap the paper around one end of a stick.
2. Ask them to secure the paper to the stick with tape.
3. When the children tire of "brushing the cobwebs off the sky," the broom can be turned into the old woman in the rhyme. Have the kids paint a face on the handle of the broom, then cut out paper arms and tape them to the handle. The children can also paint clothes on the handle to decorate as they choose.

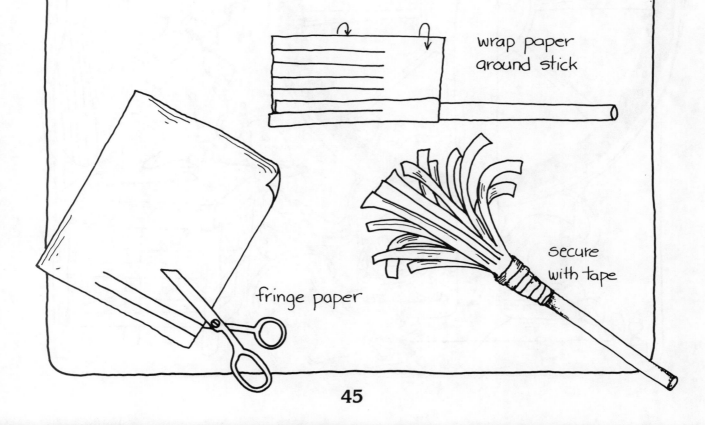

wrap paper around stick

fringe paper

secure with tape

Six Little Mice

Six little mice sat down to spin;
Pussy passed by and she peeped in.
What are you doing, my little men?
Weaving coats for gentlemen.
Shall I come in and cut off your threads?
No, no, Mistress Pussy, you'd bite off our heads.
Oh, no I'll not; I'll help you to spin.
That may be so, but you don't come in.

Weaving

In this activity, the children weave individual wall hangings. Encourage the kids to be creative in their selection of materials.

You Will Need:
burlap (potato) sacks
feathers, yarn, fabric scraps, dried flowers, leaves, colored
    construction paper, etc.
sticks, approximately 10″ long
scissors

Here's What To Do:
1. Cut the sacks into 8″ squares.
2. Give each child a burlap square, a variety of weaving materials, and a stick. Show them how to weave the different materials through the burlap. Have them start their weaving about three inches from the top of the square.
3. When the children have completed their weaving, show them how to insert a stick by weaving it through the top of the burlap. The weaving can then be taken home and hung on a wall.

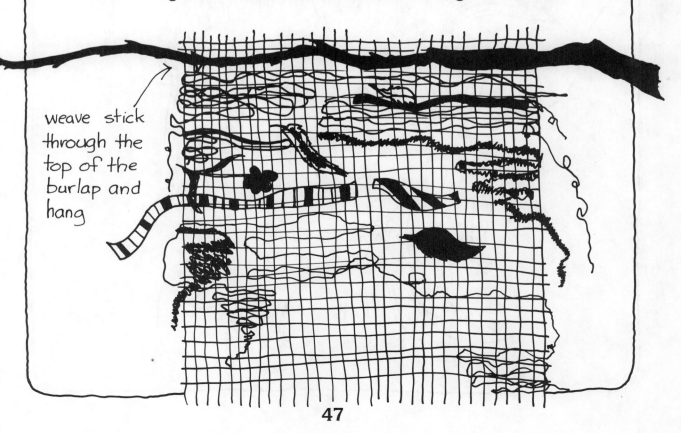

weave stick
through the
top of the
burlap and
hang

Little Nanny Button-Cap

The moon shines bright
The stars give light,
And little Nanny Button-Cap
Will come tomorrow night.

Moon and Star Mobile

The children make small mobiles to take home and hang.

You Will Need:
construction paper
string
paper punch
glitter, sequins, or water-based paints

Here's What To Do:
1. Cut one moon and two stars from the construction paper for each child.
2. Using the paper punch, punch three holes in the moon and one hole in each of the two stars as shown.
3. Give each child a moon, two stars, and some string. Have them decorate their cutouts with glitter, sequins, or paint.
4. Let the children attach the moon and stars as shown.

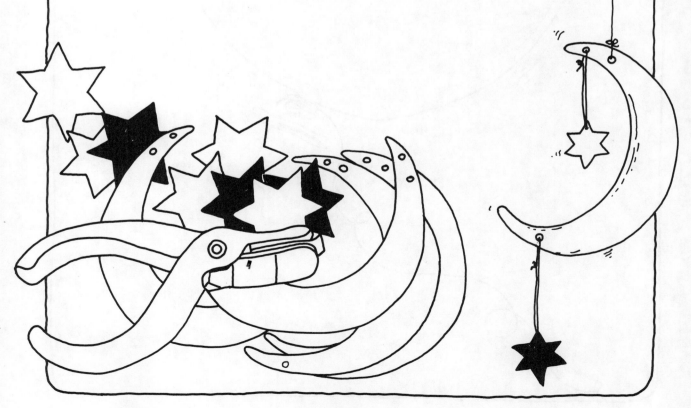

The Balloon

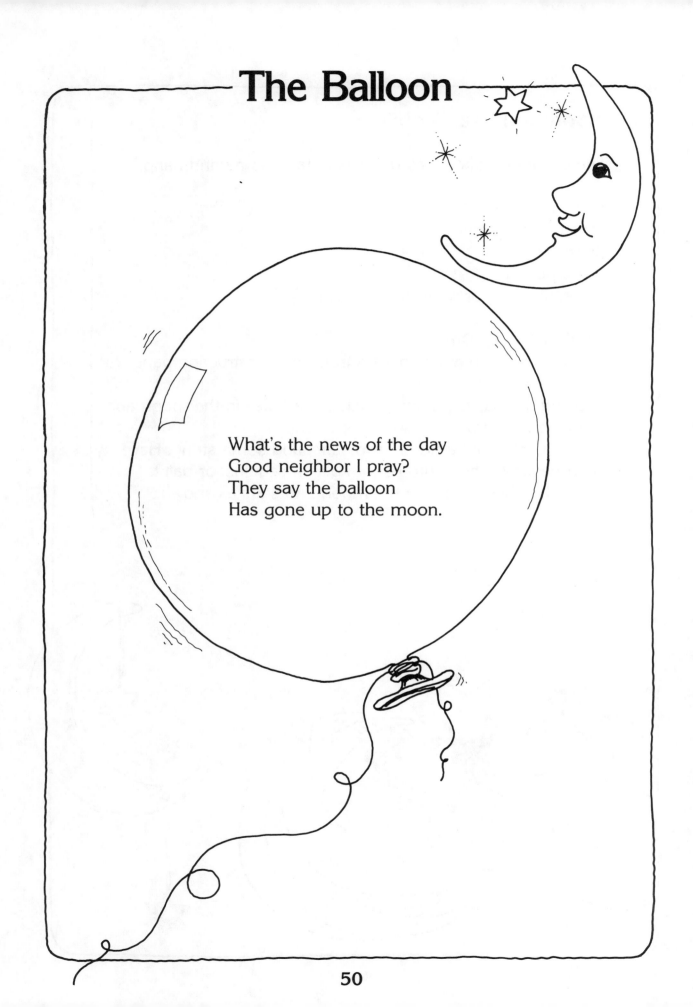

What's the news of the day
Good neighbor I pray?
They say the balloon
Has gone up to the moon.

Balloon Spaceship

The children will love this space creation—it's quite exciting during blast-off!

You Will Need:
balloons
Styrofoam cups
crayons
tissue paper strips (optional)
tape (optional)

Here's What To Do:
1. Give each child one balloon, one Styrofoam cup, and some crayons.
2. Let the children decorate their cups for a trip to the moon. Tissue streamers can be taped on for an added effect.
3. Show the children how to position a partially blown-up balloon in a cup, holding the balloon neck closed. When the kids let go, the balloons will rocket off.

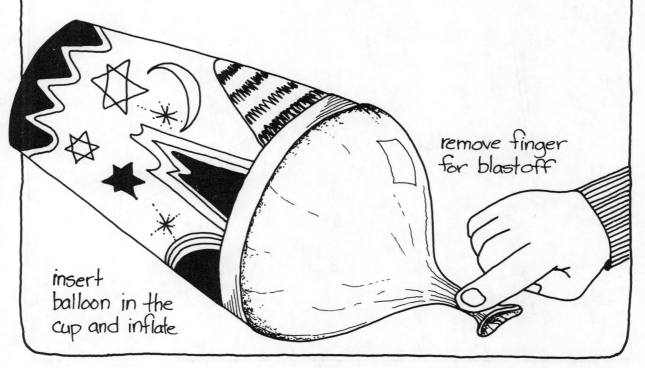

remove finger for blastoff

insert balloon in the cup and inflate

Twinkle, Twinkle, Little Star

Twinkle, twinkle, little star,
How I wonder what you are!
Up above the world so high,
Like a diamond in the sky.

Magic Wand

Individual stars can be attached to Popsicle sticks to create magic wands or wire and string can replace the sticks to make a large mobile.

You Will Need:
12″ white pipe cleaners
Popsicle sticks
glue
glitter
scissors

Here's What To Do:
1. Have each child cut a pipe cleaner in half, shaping each half into a triangle as shown. Have the kids twist the triangle ends to secure them.
2. Help the children attach the two triangles with six spots of glue, forming a six-pointed star.
3. When the glue has dried, let the kids add spots of glue to the star and dip the star in glitter.
4. When the glue has dried again, dip one point of the star in the glue and attach it to a Popsicle stick.

bend a pipe cleaner to form a triangle, twist ends to secure

add spots of glue to secure triangles together

dip point in glue and attach to stick

53

Banbury Cross

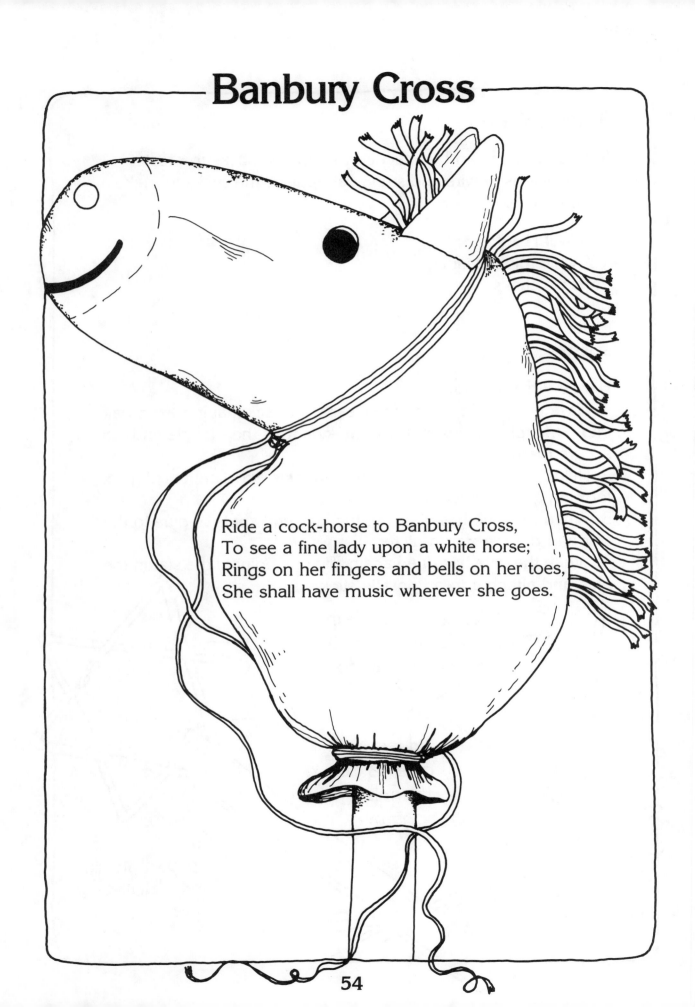

Ride a cock-horse to Banbury Cross,
To see a fine lady upon a white horse;
Rings on her fingers and bells on her toes,
She shall have music wherever she goes.

Stick Horse

The kids will have fun making their own horses to ride around the room or outside.

You Will Need:
clean white socks or small paper bags
dowels or sticks approximately 1"x30"
cotton, clean nylons, or newspaper
non-toxic felt-tip markers
heavy yarn
fabric or felt scraps
glue

Here's What To Do:
1. Ask the children to stuff a sock or bag with cotton or other stuffing material and insert the dowel about halfway in.
2. Have them use a length of yarn to tie shut the end of the sock or bag, securing it to the dowel.
3. Have the children tie another length of yarn around the stuffed sock or bag an inch or two below the top of the dowel. Then have them loop the center of a five-foot piece of yarn several times around the sock or bag at this tying point, leaving two two-foot lengths of yarn. These ends should be tied together to form a loop rein.
4. The children can glue on pieces of felt or fabric for the ears and mane.
5. Finally, let the children draw faces on the sock or bag with the markers.

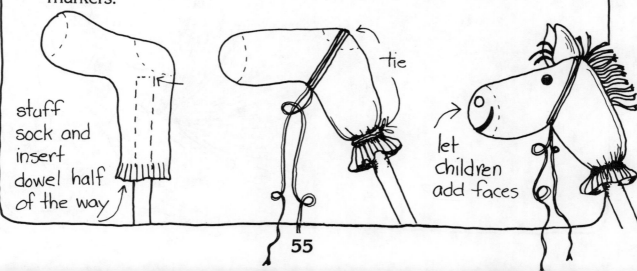

stuff sock and insert dowel half of the way

tie

let children add faces

The Winds

The south wind brings wet weather,
The north wind wet and cold together,
The west wind always brings us rain,
The east wind blows it back again.

Wind Chimes

Children can work together to create one special wind chime or each child can make his or her own.

You Will Need (for each wind chime):
coated florist or hobby wire (3 12" pieces per child)
string
bottle caps, small nuts or bolts, large paper clips, seashells, etc.
hammer and nail

Here's What To Do:
1. Help the children fold each piece of wire at the middle and twist to form a loop. Show them how to straighten the wire, loop each end, and twist to secure.
2. Have the kids attach a piece of string to each loop, joining the wires as shown.
3. Now let the children attach bottle caps, shells, and so on to the remaining strings. Use the hammer and nail to punch holes in the caps for the kids to hang.

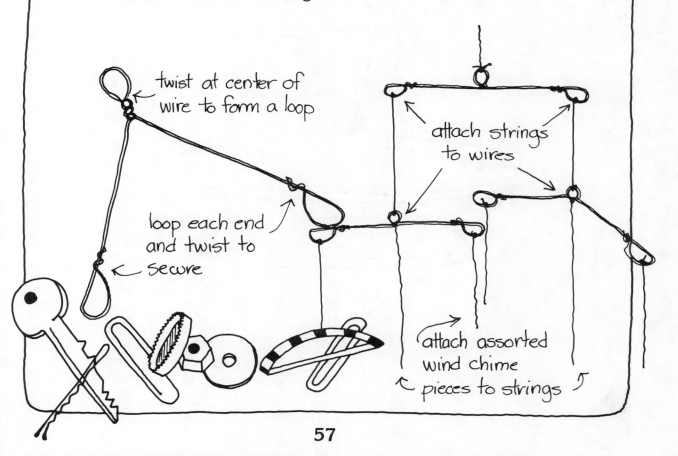

twist at center of wire to form a loop

loop each end and twist to secure

attach strings to wires

attach assorted wind chime pieces to strings

Babylon

How many miles to Babylon?
Three score miles and ten.
Can I get there by candlelight?

Yes, and back again.
If your heels are nimble and light,
You may get there by candlelight.

Candle

Help the children create beautifully decorated candles. The candles make lovely holiday gifts.

You Will Need:
small candles (approximately 2"x⅛")
paper and fabric scraps
glue
non-toxic felt-tip markers
paraffin
tweezers
coffee can
oven

Here's What To Do:
1. Give each child one candle, some scraps of paper or fabric, a marker, and a small amount of glue. Encourage the kids to decorate their candle as much as they like.
2. Melt the paraffin in a coffee can.
3. Hold each decorated candle by the wick with the tweezers and dip into the paraffin.

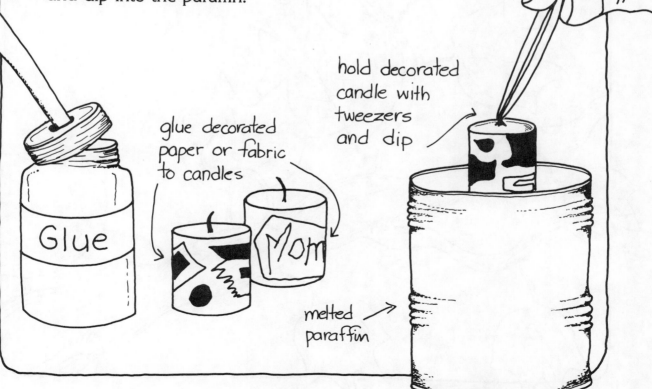

hold decorated candle with tweezers and dip

glue decorated paper or fabric to candles

Glue

melted paraffin

The Bumblebee

The bumblebee, the bumblebee,
He flew to the top of the tulip tree;
He flew to the top, but he could not stop,
For he had to get home to early tea.

The bumblebee, the bumblebee,
He flew away from the tulip tree;
But he made a mistake and flew into the lake,
And he never got home to early tea.

Pipe Cleaner Bee

These bees can fly alone or join together to make a group mobile.

You Will Need:
black pipe cleaners (four 3″ pieces per child)
yellow pipe cleaners (two 6″ pieces per child)
small, large-holed wooden beads
string

Here's What To Do:
1. Give each child one black pipe cleaner section, one yellow pipe cleaner section, and one bead.
2. Have the children loop the black pipe cleaner through the bead and twist the ends together, forming a circle (see figure 1). Tape can be used to secure ends.
3. Have the children form a figure eight with the yellow pipe cleaner, twisting the center of the figure eight to secure (see figure 2).
4. Help the kids insert the figure eight—the wings—through the circle, behind the bead—the head. Show them how to twist the black circular pipe cleaner to form the body (see figure 3).
5. Let the children attach a length of string to their bees for a buzz around the room.

1) insert black pipe cleaner through bead and twist

2) form a figure 8 with the yellow pipe cleaner

twist to secure

3) wrap the black pipe cleaner around the yellow pipe cleaner

children can make faces on the bead

A Kite

I often sit and wish that I
Could be a kite up in the sky,
And ride upon the breeze and go
Whichever way I chanced to blow.

Kite Construction

The results of this activity are colorful kites.

You Will Need:
large garbage or plastic shopping bags, white or clear
dowels or heavy cardboard strips
tape
large-eye needle
non-toxic felt-tip markers
scissors
tissue strips

Here's What To Do:
1. Have the children cut the bags into squares and decorate them with the markers.
2. Help the kids strengthen the corners of the squares with tape.
3. Now have the children position and tape the dowels or cardboard strips to the plastic as shown.
4. Have the children attach crossing pieces of string from corner to opposite corner, securing them with a knot. Check each kite to make sure the strings are taut and that the kite has a slight bow to it. Have the kids attach a tail made of tissue strips at one corner.
5. Let the kids tie a string to the front of the kite, corner to opposite corner. Have them attach a good length of string three-quarters of the way up this string and the kite is ready to fly.

tape corners
tape dowels to plastic
attach string to front of kite

Resources

de Angeli, Marguerite. *Marguerite de Angeli's Book of Nursery and Mother Goose Rhymes.* Doubleday and Co., New York, 1954.

Editors of Sunset Books and Magazine. *Children's Crafts.* Lane Publishing Co., Menlo Park, CA, 1976.

Fiarotta, Phyllis and Noel. *Snips and Snails and Walnut Whales.* Workman Publishing Co., New York, 1977.

Iveson, Barbara, ed. *The Faber Book of Nursery Verse.* Faber and Faber, London, 1983.

Johnson, June. *838 Ways to Amuse a Child.* Collier Books, New York, 1960.

Offen, Hilda. *A Treasury of Mother Goose.* Simon and Schuster, New York, 1984.

Sutherland, Zena, ed. *The Arbuthnot Anthology of Children's Literature.* Scott, Foresman, Chicago, 1976.

Warren, Jean. *Story Time.* Monday Morning Books, Palo Alto, CA, 1984.